*To* Brad + Leah.

①

# BETWS-Y-COED

*A*
*Pictorial Trip Down*
*Memory Lane*

by
Ray Sandiford

Edited by:
G. L. J. Kershaw

Thank-you for visiting
Betws-y-coed :
A Pictorial Trip Down
Memory Lane Exhibition.

Ray Sandiford.
19th, August 1992.

*First Edition*
*Published in Wales 1992*
*by*
*Country Cottage Publications*
*Bryn Tirion, Betws-y-coed,*
*Gwynedd, Wales, LL24 0DA.*


*Copyright © by Ray Sandiford*
*1992*
*ISBN: 0-9519197-0-9*

*Printed and bound by*
*Gwasg Carreg Gwalch, Capel Garmon,*
*Llanrwst, Gwynedd, Wales.*

## DEDICATION

*Shuffling and reshuffling the pages of the book
has been made much easier by the dedication of a dear friend
who has worked very hard by my side.*

*Much love and appreciation.*

*Thank You, Kirsch*

"Every year more people come hither for rest, for pure air, and for the scenic panoramas, all of which can be enjoyed in perfection, by lovers of quietude. There is none of the whirl and rush and racket of the popular watering places, and even the day trippers are content to wander about and watch the cloud-capped hills, and the foaming torrents, and the roaring falls to be found all around. Artists come in hundreds, and in the season the whole neighbourhood is thickly dotted with their great white umbrellas and the little white tents, underneath which their easels are shielded from the glare."

**JOHN HEYWOOD**

John Heywood's Illustrated Guide, *Betws-y-coed and the Conwy Valley*, 1930s.

# CONTENTS

# ACKNOWLEDGEMENTS

The author would like to thank Gina Kershaw for her patience in helping with the editing of this book and his mother for the poem on Betws-y-coed.

He would also like to thank all the people in the village of Betws-y-coed for all their moral support. With a special thanks in memory to John French Pierce.

He would also like to thank Tattum Insurance, Llanrwst, for kindly letting the author use their photocopier.

Not forgetting all the Postcard Publishers without whose kind permission to reproduce this book would not have been possible. The number relates to its position in the book:-

VALENTINES
(7,8,19,20,30,39,40,42,44,45,52,54,55,57,62,65,76,77,79,80,
81,82,86,87,96,100,103,104,105)
A.W.H. (95)
ALFRED T. HUGHES (32,74,75)
BAURS SERIES (2,3,4,5,6,31)
HANNAH JONES & SONS (1)
HUGH LANG & CO. (49)
J. BURROW & CO.LTD. (67)
J. LLOYD (13)
JUDGES POSTCARDS LTD., HASTINGS (16,58,63,90)
MINIATURE NOVEL SERIES (56)
O. EVANS (61)
PHOTO PRECISION LTD. (47,53)
PICTORIAL STATIONERY CO.LTD. (27,37,50,71)
RAPHAEL TUCK & SONS LTD. (97)
RELIABLE SERIES (15)
S. M. GIBSON & CO. (28,29,66)
SHARPLES PHOTOS (22)
SIMPSONS THE PRINTERS (34)
PHOTOCHROM CO.LTD. (14,25,26,43,64)
R.A.P. CO.LTD. (12,23,24)
VINE SERIES (17)
WYNDHAM (91)
REFLEX G. W. (33)

# Introduction

In the 1700s, Betws-y-coed consisted mainly of farm houses scattered around the hillsides, with a small hamlet around the Pont-y-pair bridge. The Inns around the bridge would have been *The Swan* and *The Hand*. Some of the houses around the bridge being called Tyn-y-ffynnon, Pont-y-pair, Crosskeys and Rhyd Lygwy.

To the east of the bridge would have been another group of houses around The Royal Oak which was quite near the old church. The rest of the area would have consisted of small farms such as Trawsafon, Gartheryr, Llannerch Elsi, Mynydd Bychan and Cwmlannerch.

The village would have been very peaceful until the early 1800s when the Capel Curig Turnpike Trust built a road through for the Irish Mail Coach. This is when people started thinking what a nice place Betws-y-coed is.

The artists and fishermen soon got to know about Betws, they then came in droves.

In the 1860s, the railway came to Betws, bringing more people in. The little old church of St Michael's could not fit all the people in for the church service so they built the new St Mary's church.

Even the hotels could not cope with the influx of the people, down came the old houses, up went the modern hotels.

Then the motorists started arriving, so up went more hotels, with the existing hotels being extended. By the early 1900s a new Betws had been born.

Today, if you went up to Clogwyn Cyrau and looked down on Betws, it looks like a bee's hive with all the coaches, cars and motorbikes buzzing in and out.

What would the old people of Betws say if they could "see it now"?

# MY LOVE FOR BETWS

How I wish I could have seen "Old Betws", the little village with the small houses and inns. To have been here with all the artists. To have seen the mail coaches rattle by.

Alas, all we can catch of the days gone by is what some people have left to show us what it was like. We should be proud of the late artists and engravers, names like W. Radclyffe (engraver), Munn (artist), D. Cox (artist), T. Creswick (artist), and the postcard publishers for leaving us with some of their memoirs of how "Old Betws" used to be.

I would like to point out that the adverts advertising the hotels etc., in the postcard section are old ones and that before 1950 Betws-y-coed was spelt with the double 'T'. There is a section at the back of the book between pages 76-78 which lists current places to stay, eat & drink, and places of interest. If you visit any of the 'new' after visiting the 'old' in the book, please tell them you saw them first in your Pictorial Trip Down Memory Lane.

I hope this book gives you plenty of enjoyment — as much as it gave me collecting the postcards for you to see.

*R. Sandiford*

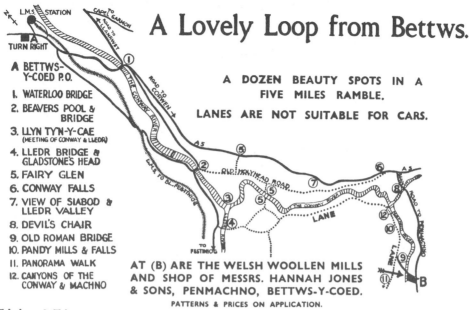

# A Lovely Loop from Bettws.

A DOZEN BEAUTY SPOTS IN A
FIVE MILES RAMBLE.

LANES ARE NOT SUITABLE FOR CARS.

A BETTWS-Y-COED P.O.

1. WATERLOO BRIDGE
2. BEAVERS POOL & BRIDGE
3. LLYN TY'N-Y-CAE (MEETING OF CONWAY & LLEDR)
4. LLEDR BRIDGE & GLADSTONE'S HEAD
5. FAIRY GLEN
6. CONWAY FALLS
7. VIEW OF SIABOD & LLEDR VALLEY
8. DEVIL'S CHAIR
9. OLD ROMAN BRIDGE
10. PANDY MILLS & FALLS
11. PANORAMA WALK
12. CANYONS OF THE CONWAY & MACHNO

AT (B) ARE THE WELSH WOOLLEN MILLS
AND SHOP OF MESSRS. HANNAH JONES
& SONS, PENMACHNO, BETTWS-Y-COED.

PATTERNS & PRICES ON APPLICATION.

*Telephones & Telegrams: Jones, 52 Bettws-y-Coed.*       *Registered at Stationer's Hall*

## A LOVELY LOOP FROM BETWS

Let's go on a Loop Round Betws and see some of the changes and how it used to be.

We start at the Waterloo Bridge [see card 7] and take the A5 towards Llangollen. As we leave the Waterloo Bridge we will pass Tŷ Gwyn Hotel (on left) which used to be called the Blue Bird Cafe [see cards 10,11,12].

Continue along the A5 and after a while you should see some beautiful views over the Lledr Valley and Moel Siabod. A little further along you will pass the Silver Fountain Inn (on left) which was once the Conwy Falls Cottage [see card 13]. Carry on until you see a sign for Penmachno B4406 (on right) and turn down this road and you will come to what is now called the Conwy Falls Cafe [see card 14] where you can park up and visit the Conwy Falls [see card 15].

Back onto the B4406 and head towards Penmachno. Your next stop will be Penmachno Woollen Mills (on right). Inside you will be able to see the Weaving Machines at work. Now leave the car park, turn left, and take the first lane on your left down to the Bridge at the side of the Mill and you will be able to see the Roman Bridge [see card 16] downstream and the Waterfalls up-stream. Continue down this road until you come to the first house on your left which is Pandy Mill [see cards 17,18]. Follow the road for quite a distance and when you reach a row of cottages on your left, take the right fork, go over the old Lledr Bridge [see card 19] and turn right along A470 to Betws-y-coed. You pass a derelict Toll House (on right) and soon approach the Beaver Bridge [see card 20] which you go across. There you can park near the Fairy Glen Hotel and walk to the Fairy Glen itself [see card 21] but beware when going down to the glen as it can be a bit dangerous. Once visited, we carry on along the A470 and pass Coed-y-Celyn Hall (on left) [see cards 23,24].

At the junction turn left and head back to Betws-y-coed over the Waterloo Bridge. You will pass the Waterloo Motel (on left). We then pass the Glan Aber [see card 30-32] and Gwydyr Hotels [see cards 33-35]. Turn right at the traffic lights towards the Railway Station to park your car up.

We then go to the Station [see card 36] and over the Railway Bridge. You can visualise what it was like in its busier days. The Railway Museum used to be a Goods Warehouse. Cross the miniature railway lines, through the small gate and you will come to the original parish church, St Michael's and All Angels, [see cards 37,38]. It's well worth having a look around the Church Yard. With your back to the Church Bell Tower, to the left and behind you is the Suspension Bridge [see cards 39,40] and the Church Pool, and to the left and down the road you can see Henllys Guest House, which used to be the Court House. Make your way back through the Church Yard to the entrance you came through and turn right to the Caravan Park where the Riverside Tea Gardens [see card 41] used to be. Follow the road along the riverside to Betws-y-coed Golf Club. The old house is where the Gas Works used to be. Follow the footpath along the perimeter of the Golf Course when you will come to the Stepping Stones (on right at the 17th Tee) [see card 42]. Further along the footpath you will come to the meeting of the Waters, the Conwy and Llugwy Rivers. As you continue along, under the railway bridge, you will pass the Royal Oak Farm (on right) which used to be the Royal Oak Mill [see card 43]. Just on the left of the farm is where the farm buildings would have been which have now been converted into living accommodation and the Motor Car Museum. Go through the gate at the end of the footpath and on your left is the Tourist Information Centre which used to be the Royal Oak Stables.

Turn right towards the Royal Oak Hotel [see cards 45-47] in whose lounge you can see their famous sign which David Cox painted [see card 48]. You are now in the heart of the village. You will pass guest houses and shops and if you look on the outside stonework on some of the buildings you will see their original names and see if it is still the same. See how many of them you can find in the old postcards.

Head along up the road taking the righthand footpath to the Pont-y-pair Bridge [see cards 63], stopping on the bridge to admire Fir Tree Island [see card 53]. Bear right into Mill Street [see cards 55,56] keeping on the righthand side passing Bryn Afon [see card 61]. Further along you will pass the cottages Preswylfa and Hyfrydle where the Hand Inn used to be. When you reach the last house on your right, cross the road and continue up it again. You will see a white dwelling on your right, Bodlondeb, which used to be the Miners Arms Inn in the 1890s. Further along is the Y Felin flats which used to be the Albert Mill [see card 44].

On the right, just before you re-cross over the Pont-y-pair Bridge, is the Memorial Hall and Bryn-y-Bont [see cards 51,52].

Turn right past the Pont-y-pair Stores and continue along the righthand footpath, passing The Gallery which used to be a school, Upstairs Downstairs which used to be a family grocers, Llys Caradog [see advert on Page 49] until you reach Bryn Mawr Chapel (on left). Turn back towards the village and look out for the following houses Tan-y-Marian [see card 66], Riverside Restaurant which used to be The Ancaster Hotel, and Caban-y-Pair which used to be Ancaster Milk Bar [see cards 67,68], Glan 'R-Afon Cottage [see card 69], Pont-y-pair Hotel which used to be The Swan and the Masonic Hall [see cards 64,70], Climber and Rambler which used to be Llugwy Cottage [see card 72]. Craft-centre Cymru which was many things including Llugwy Tea Rooms [see cards 74,75]. Just past the Royal Oak's car park is St Mary's Church [see cards 79,80]. Further along the A5 is Tan Lan Restaurant which used to be Tan Lan Temperance Hotel [see card 85]. You can now cross the road at the traffic lights and head back to your car.

Now you make your way up the A5 towards Bangor, passing the hotels and guest houses where you have just been. When you pass the Crosskeys and Guests Houses (on left) [see card 88]. You will also pass some more houses [see card 89], when you will come to the Miners Bridge Inn which used to be The Oakfield [see card 92]. You are now at Pentre Du [see card 90]. Park up and cross the A5 and look up the river and you will see Miners Bridge [see card 93]. Jane Jones used to have a Stall at the entrance to the bridge [see card 91]. You can walk up to the bridge and look at the lovely views.

Back to the car to carry on up the A5 going past the Swallow Falls Hotel on your left. After about a further mile you will cross a bridge and on the right-hand corner is the Ugly House [see card 94] which you can visit. Turn the car round and go back down the A5 to the Swallow Falls Hotel [see card 96] and visit the Swallow Falls themselves [see cards 100,101]. Now you know why people call Betws-y-coed "THE PARADISE OF WALES".

# BETWS-Y-COED

**LOOP TOUR**                                                          Nos. 2, 3, 4, 5 & 6

In its heyday, some of the hotels had horse drawn omnibuses — The Waterloo, Glan Aber, Gwydyr and The Royal Oak. Here you can see some of the carriages and omnibuses taking the people on a loop tour round Snowdon.

Scene 4 on Loop Tour: Cobdens Hotel, Capel Curig.

2.

Scene 2 on Loop Tour: Bettws-y-Coed.

3.

Scene 1 on Loop Tour: Under the Oak, Waterloo Hotel, Bettws-y-Coed.

4.

Scene 3 on Loop Tour: On the way to Swallow Falls.

5.

Scene 5 on Loop Tour: Near Ugly House, Capel Curig.

6.

7.

## WATERLOO BRIDGE (Y BONT HAEARN) THE IRON BRIDGE　　　　　　Nos. 7 & 8

Waterloo Bridge built by Thomas Telford in 1815, the same year as the Battle of Waterloo. It was built to improve the travelling for the people between London and Dublin. The bridge can be found on the A5 and spans the River Conwy. It is decorated with the Leek, Rose, Shamrock and Thistle, being the emblems of Wales, England, Ireland and Scotland — (top). The A.A. Man on Patrol in left of postcard (bottom). Those were the days when he would salute you if your car was displaying the A.A. Badge!

8.

9.

# "CRAIG-Y-DDERWEN"

## PRIVATE HOTEL

This Hotel is delightfully situated by the side of the River Conway near Waterloo Bridge. Beautiful views. Electric Light. Open Fires. Billiards Excellently appointed. H. & C. in all Bedrooms. Tariff on application.

---

**TELEPHONE 71**                  **Garage for 8 Cars**

A.A. and R.A.C. Appointed

11.

## TŶ GWYN and BLUE BIRD                                    Nos. 10, 11 & 12

George Harrison, a local artist, lived at the Tŷ Gwyn in the 1880s. The Tŷ Gwyn changed to the Blue Bird Tea Rooms in the 1920s and has since reverted back to the Tŷ Gwyn Hotel and Restaurant.

12.

**CONWAY FALLS COTTAGE**                                                    No. 13

These cottages used to be a small coaching inn. Today, the establishment is known as the Silver Fountain Inn and is one and a half miles south east of Betws-y-coed on the A5.

**CONWAY FALLS SNACK BAR**                                                  No. 14

Today, where the Snack Bar used to be, is the Conway Falls Café. This is where you can park up to go and see the Conway Falls for a slight admission charge.

15.

CONWAY FALLS, with its Salmon Ladder, is well worth seeing. Situate in one of the most romantic spots in North Wales, two miles from Bettws-y-Coed, half-a-mile from Fairy Glen, along a lovely green lane—a glen all the way—from whence is obtained a magnificent view of the noted Lledr Valley, with Moel Siabod rising majestically in the background.

**ROMAN BRIDGE**  *(JUDGES POSTCARDS LTD. HASTINGS)*  **No. 16**

The artists loved to paint this quaint old bridge which was an old pack horse bridge. It was built in A.D. 200. Just upstream is the Machno Falls at the side of the Penmachno Woollen Mill.

17.

## PANDY MILL

Extract from a 1905 Guide Book, "Continuing the walk from the Roman Bridge, in about 300 yards you will come to Pandy Mill and Falls, the surroundings of which have been somewhat altered by the clearing away of several quaint old out buildings, and the erection of a lodging house, but the Falls and Mill still remain intact".

Not much remains of the Mill today, but well worth a look to capture the days gone by.

18.

**PONT-AR-LEDR BRIDGE**                                                No. 19

The bridge carries the old road to Penmachno over the river Lledr. Built in 1468, attributed to Hywel Saer (*the Mason*).

**PONT-YR-AFANC** (*Beaver Bridge*)                                    No. 20

Pont-yr-Afanc, built by the Capel Curig Turn Pike Trust in 1803, crosses the River Conwy by a nearly semi-circular arch, 68 feet in span by 23 feet wide. The Irish Mail Coach, which travelled via Chester and Conwy, diverted through Betws in 1808 over the Beaver Bridge and up the old road into the village.

21.

## DAY OUTING AT BETWS                                    Nos. 21 & 22

The railroads and coaches brought the people in droves to Betws-y-coed. The hackney carriages were waiting at the station ready to take the visitors to their destinations.
The postcard above is a group of people at the Fairy Glen in the year 1913.
Underneath, the postcard shows a party of people at the Pont-y-pair Bridge. The card is dated 1907.

22.

23.

## COED-Y-CELYN

Coed-y-Celyn (*Wood of Holly*) is just off the A470 road to Dolwyddelan, about half a mile from the Waterloo Bridge. The property, at this previous time, belonged to Mr H. Byrd. He also owned the Blue Bird Tea Rooms.

24.

**MIN AFON**                                                             **No. 25**

In the 1900s this house belonged to Alfred E. Rodewald, a Liverpool Merchant, who founded the Liverpool Music Society. His friend, Sir Edward Elgar, finalised the "Apostles" in 1903 at Min Afon and also composed *Land of Hope & Glory*. The house is now a private residence owned by Doctor Chown who was a local practitioner until he retired.

**BEAVER GROVE (1910s)**                                                 **No.26**

Advert stated "Is charmingly situated with extensive grounds overlooking River Conwy. The rooms are comfortable and well furnished and most of them large. Board Residence or Apartments. Milk, eggs and vegetables supplied. Water and sanitation perfect. Motor House, Stabling, etc. Highest references". Proprietress: Mrs Thomas. (This house is now a private dwelling).

27.

# DAVID J. OWEN,
## FAMILY GROCER,
## BAKER & CONFECTIONER,
### WILLOUGHBY HOUSE, BETTWS-Y-COED.

Genuine HOME-MADE BREAD Daily.  Huntley & Palmer's BISCUITS.
JAMS, JELLIES, MARMALADES, SAUCES, PICKLES. &c.
HOME-CURED HAMS AND BACON.

### D. J. OWEN,
#### WILLOUGHBY HOUSE,
## Family & Temperance Hotel,

Within Three Minutes' Walk of the Railway Station, with splendid
Mountain, Wood and River Views.  Moderate Tariff.

**THE FERNS (1910s)**                                                    No. 28

Advert stated "Two large size sitting-rooms and five bedrooms, close to Railway Station, standing in its own grounds." Proprietress: Mrs Hughes.
This house in on the A5.

**MAELGWYN HOUSE**                                                       No. 29

Advert stated "With or without Board. House pleasantly situated overlooking the River Conwy. Six bedrooms and three sitting rooms. Bath — hot or cold. Central for fishing on the Rivers Llugwy, Conwy and Lledr".
This house is on the A5.

# HOME FARM PRODUCE

# Glan Aber Hotel

30.

GLAN ABER HOTEL, BETTWS-Y-COED.

First-class Old Established Residential and Tourist Hotel, centrally situated. Every Comfort. Open all the year round.

Electric light throughout.        Spacious Garage.
Motors and carriages for hire. Fishing tickets obtainable.
Close to tennis and croquet.
Officially appointed R.A.C., A.A., M.U., A.C.U., C.T.C.
Personal Supervision.

*Apply for terms—*

## Mrs. A. EVANS, Resident Proprietress

Wheelers Coach, leaving Glan Aber Hotel, Bettws-y-Coed.

31.

## GLAN ABER HOTEL                                      Nos. 30, 31 & 32

Around the 1900s this hotel had 11 horses, 3 carriages, 2 omnibuses and 8 traps. A 3 horse break would meet every train arriving to take the tourists to the Swallow Falls and Fairy Glen. Here you can see the Wheelers Coach getting ready to start its journey around Snowdonia.

32.

The Gwydyr Hotel, Bettws-y-Coed, N. Wales.

33.

# The Gwydyr Hotel,

### Bettws=y=Coed.

The above High-class Hotel is beautifully situated, and combines every comfort and attention.

## Private and Public Rooms.
### Ladies' Drawing Room.

POSTING.   LAWN TENNIS.

Tickets for Fishing in the neighbouring rivers and lakes may be had at the Hotel.

**The Misses FAICHNEY, Proprietresses.**

34.

## GWYDYR HOTEL                                    Nos. 33, 34 & 35

Ebiniser Faichney came to Betws in the 1830s. The house was then a small private dwelling. By the 1880s the house had been extended a couple of times and was then running as the Gwydyr Hotel. When Ebiniser died, his daughters then ran the hotel. Miss Violet Smith, who ran the hotel until the 1980s, was the grand-daughter from the Faichney sisters. Her father, Thomas Connell Smith, who ran the hotel in the 1920s, managed to get the lease for the hotel to fish on some of the nearby rivers. The hotel is now run by the Wainwright family who still enjoy the fishing rights.

35.

36.

# L.M.S. Railway Station
# Refreshment Rooms and Cafe

### BETTWS-Y-COED

are now opened under Private Management.

### Grocer and Provision Dealer

\* \* \*

*LUNCHEONS and TEAS*

*HOME-MADE CAKES :: ICES*

*TOBACCO & CIGARETTES*

\* \* \*

### DELIVERIES TO ALL PARTS OF BETTWS-Y-COED.

## PARKING GROUND FOR CARS

Mrs. VAUGHAN HUGHES, *Proprietress.*

TEL.: 50 Bettws-y-Coed.

Bettws-y-Coed       The Old Church.

37.

## ST MICHAEL'S AND ALL ANGELS           Nos. 37 & 38

The old church, dated around the 14th century, originally was a simple rectangle building, but in 1843 a large transept was added at the north side and a vestry at the south east side. The old church had a cross on the bell tower, as you can see in the photo. If you take a look at the bell tower, you will see where the rope has cut into the stone. Also, in the top photo, you will see the sundial that went missing in 1966. In the grounds of the church are some yew trees which add character to all the surroundings.

Bettws-y-coed Old Church and Yew Tree.

38.

39.

## ENGINEERS AND SUSPENSION BRIDGES                    Nos. 39 & 40

The Engineers Bridge (above) was built by the Royal Engineers in the First World War and is sited at the side of the old church, spanning the church pool (the River Conwy). This card was sold by Tan Lan, proprietor was a Mr Thomas Hughes, in 1917. The bridge was swept away by floods in 1928.
The Suspension Bridge (below) was built in its place in 1930 and has become an alternative way to cross the Conwy to the stepping stones.

40.

41.

# RIVERSIDE TEA GARDENS.

The floral display of Roses and Rock
Plants is magnificent and the beauty
of the Gardens unsurpassed in the
Principality. Meals·are served in an up-
to-date

# CAFE and RESTAURANT

with promptness, and the food supplied
is of the best—at moderate prices.

## LUNCHEONS.  TEAS.

LAWN TENNIS.    WIRELESS MUSIC.
BOWLS.

Seating capacity 500 persons.

Ideal for large parties.

*The Stepping Stones, Bettws-y-Coed*

## THE STEPPING STONES                                                No. 42

The Stepping Stones would have been one of the earliest ways of crossing the river. They would have been put there so people could get to the old church easily. The steps are downstream from the church. Here, in the postcard, you can see just how easy it was to cross in the early 1900s and how good the steps looked. Were the steps vandalised due to a lady drowning in 1912 when she slipped off them, or have they been disturbed by the fast flowing currents of the river? Whichever it is, anybody trying to cross now will find it a very difficult task to undertake, but the stones are still a big tourist attraction.

## ROYAL OAK MILL                                                   No. 43

The Mill originated from the 14th century. The undershot wheel was used mostly for making butter and at one time belonged to the Royal Oak Hotel. The Mill is situated at the backside of the Information Centre.

## ALBERT MILL                                                      No. 44

Albert Mill was situated in Mill Street in 1886. Edward Roberts was the miller. In 1917, Robert Roberts was the miller and you can see him sitting in front of the mill wheel in the postcard. The overshot wheel ran from water taken from the River Llugwy. The spent water was channelled under Mill Street, back into the Llugwy.

# 𝕽𝖔𝖞𝖆𝖑 𝕺𝖆𝖐 𝕳𝖔𝖙𝖊𝖑

## BETTWS-Y-COED

"The Sanctuary in the Woods"

45.

46.

## ROYAL OAK HOTEL          Nos. 45, 46 & 47

The Royal Oak Hotel started as a small white washed building in the 1700s. In 1813, Robert and Mary Williams were the landlords, until 1817 when Edward and Margaret Roberts took over the business. When Edward died, his son Robert became landlord and must have been the first one in the new Royal Oak Hotel and Posting House which was built in 1861. Unfortunately, due to ill health he died soon after and his daughters carried on the business. In 1881 Edward and Louisa Pullan were the landlords and were quite a wealthy family who owned a lot of property in the village. When Edward died he left everything to his three daughters, but his son, Frank, managed the hotel. Money problems hit the Pullan daughters in the 1930s and the liquidators put the hotel on the market in 1937. By this date only one daughter was still alive, Hetty, but died the year after due to ill health.

47.

Royal Oak Hotel,
Bettws-y-coed.

## ROYAL OAK SIGN                                             No. 48

The Royal Oak Sign, which is now hung in the hotel's lounge, represents Charles the Second hiding in the oak tree at Boscobel. The oak tree, painted by the artist — David Cox, is believed to be situated near the Royal Oak Farm where he also stayed.

DAVID COX — 1783-1859 — ARTIST

    1783 — Born at Deritend, Birmingham
    1805 — First came to North Wales
    1808 — Married Mary Ragg
    1844 — Stayed at Betws for the first time
    1845 — Wife, Mary Cox, died
    1847 — He painted the Royal Oak Sign
    1856 — Came to Betws for the last time
    1859 — David Cox died at Harborne

In 1849, David Cox wrote to a friend of his who was staying at the Royal Oak Hotel, hoping that he was comfortable and that he would look at and remember the sign that he had painted and that it would probably need retouching since it was two years since it was painted.

BETTWS - Y - COED. The Post Office.

## THE POST OFFICE (1903)                                     No. 49

The old Post Office, now the Craftcentre Cymru situated on the A5, was also a grocers, bookseller, stationer and Italian warehouse. The postmistress was Miss Jane Jones. Deliveries were — 7 a.m. and 4 p.m. Despatches were — 10.20 a.m., 6.15 p.m., 7.50 p.m — Summer.

Bettws-y-Coed. Village Street

## VILLAGE STREET                                             No. 50

Above left is the Plas Derwen and the Fairhaven Hotels. The street scene is looking up towards Pont-y-pair Bridge.

**BRYN-Y-BONT**                                                                 No. 51

This postcard shows Bryn-y-Bont before the Memorial Hall was built next to it.

**BRYN-Y-BONT & THE MEMORIAL HALL**                                             No.52

On the top centre of the postcard is a small house, Bryn-y-Bont, next to the big Memorial Hall. Not much is known about its history, but I think that it has something to do with the Wynn family from the Gwydyr Castle. At that time, could it have had a connection with the bridge? It is one of the oldest buildings in Betws. The Memorial Hall opened in 1929. In the 1930s they started a Cinema there. On Saturday, March 15th, the first film to be shown was a Metro Goldwyn picture — *Napoleon*. Prices for the first performance were 8 pence, 1 shilling for the second, and both of the houses were full.

## FIR TREE ISLAND & FALLS                                  No. 53

In August and September, people gather on the Pont-y-pair Bridge to look at the salmon leaping the Falls. It is a spectacular sight to see. So, also, are the lights on Fir Tree Island when they are lit up in December for Christmas time, which adds a really warm welcome to the visitors.

## LLUGWY COTTAGES                                          No. 54

The changing face of the old Llugwy Cottages. In the postcard the building consisted of a café but at a later day, the council had their offices there. Now, the building is the Climber and Rambler.

## MILL STREET (PENTRE-FELIN)                     No. 55

The old road leading to Llanrwst. Not much has changed. Albert Mill is still there but it has been converted into flats. The card was posted from Betws in the year 1921.

## MILL STREET                                    No. 56

Mill Street, looking towards Pont-y-pair Bridge.

**THE WOODS**                                                    No. 57

The Woods and Still Pool just at the side of the Pont-y-pair Bridge. A place where people come to sit awhile and look at the beauty that surrounds the bridge.

**THE WOODS**   *(JUDGES POSTCARDS LTD. HASTINGS)*              No. 58

A view from the woods looking across to the cottages of Glan Rafon, Tegfan and what is now the Caban-y-Pair Café.

**HAFANEDD** (1910s)                                                             **No. 59**

Advert stated "Comfortable apartments with or without board, sunny all winter, large rooms, stands in own grounds, newly built and all latest improvements, sanitary arrangements perfect". Proprietress: Mrs Lloyd Jones. Now called the Hafan. (This house is now a private dwelling).

COEDCYNHELIER,
BETTWS-Y-COED.

60.

61.

## NATIONAL SCHOOL FOR BOYS                                                        No. 62

In the centre of the postcard, you can see the National School for boys which was demolished to make way for the Memorial Hall. The other building, on the right of the card, is Bryn Afon.

**PONT-Y-PAIR BRIDGE**   *(JUDGES POSTCARDS LTD. HASTINGS)*   No. 63

Pont-y-pair Bridge carries the old road to Llanrwst and Conwy — *The Bridge of the Cauldron*. It is constructed of five arches, the middle one spans the River Llugwy. The bridge was designed and partly built by a native mason named Hywel, who died about 1470 before his work was completed.
Inigo Jones, the great architect of the first half of the seventeenth century, widened the upstream side of the river at a later date.

**MASONIC HALL**   No. 64

Masons in Betws! The original site of the Masonic Hall housed a small inn called the Swan where David Cox, the artist, stayed before making the Royal Oak his headquarters. After the inn was demolished a hotel was built, again called the Swan, and this was run by Mrs Atkinson in the 1880s. In the 1890s-1900 the Masons acquired the building for their headquarters. When they disbanded, the new name of the Pont-y-pair Hotel was born.

48

65.

Tan-y-Marian, Bettws-y-Coed.

66.

67.

# THE ANCASTER

*( The Restaurant of Comfort )*

*MODERN · MODERATE TERMS · VISITORS AND TOURISTS CATERED FOR—BED AND BREAKFAST, OR BY THE WEEK*

*Garage · Central-near Pont-y-Pair · Tel. 72*

68.

The Ancaster Hotel now the Riverside Hotel.
The Ancaster Milk Bar now the Caban-y-pair Café.

1, GLAN 'R-AFON COTTAGE, BETTWS-Y-COED.

*23·3·17*

*Dear Annie*

*Just a line or two*

69.

# WILLIAM WILLIAMS,
## Practical Tailor,
## Outfitter & Woollen Draper.

HATS, SCARVES, TIES, COLLARS, SHIRTS.
*Scotch Tweeds in great variety.*

*WEST OF ENGLAND CLOTHS.*

*Gentlemen's own Materials Made-up. Fit and Style
Guaranteed.*

☞ PLEASE NOTE THE ADDRESS—

## GLANRAFON,
(NEAR THE "SWAN HOTEL,")

# BETTWS-Y-COED.

52

*26: May 1913*

PONT-Y-PAIR HOTEL
BETTWS-Y-COED

70.

# PONT-Y-PAIR HOTEL
BETTWS-Y-COED            (*Fully Licensed*)

Good and reasonable accommodation for
your holidays. Luncheons, Teas, Dinners
and Snacks always available. Five
minutes from Station. Every comfort.

*Telephone* 20             *Mr. H. TRIPP, Proprietor*

71.

*Aug 1905*

*Llugwy Cottage) Bettws y Coed Nth Wales*

72.

# Llugwy Cottage

Overlooking the celebrated PONT-Y-PAIR BRIDGE.

## Luncheons, Dinners, or Teas.

APARTMENTS with or without Board.

ACCOMMODATION for CYCLISTS.

PROPRIETRESS: **Mrs. LLOYD JONES.**

PONT-Y-PAIR AND LLUGWY COTTAGE, BETTWS-Y-COED

**TOLL HOUSE & GATES**       **No. 73**

In the postcard you can see the old Toll House facing the cottages where the Toll Gates used to be. The Toll House was knocked down around the 1900s.

74.

## LLUGWY TEA ROOMS (1920s)                                    Nos. 74 & 75

Advert stated "Accommodation for parties, close to parking place". Proprietress: Miss Atkinson.
Originated as the Post Office, then changed its use to the Postcard Palace, then to the Llugwy Tea Rooms
and is now Craftcentre Cymru.

75.

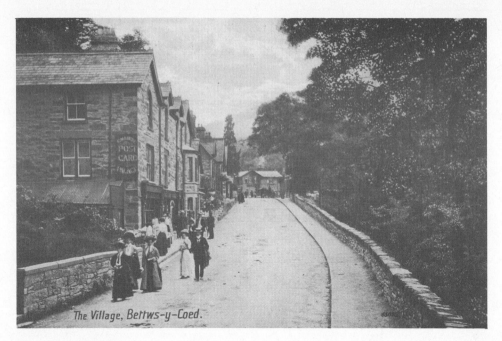

The Village, Bettws-y-Coed.

**THE VILLAGE STREET**                                                    **No. 76**

The Post Office has moved and the Postcard Palace has taken its place. The year is around 1917. The view is looking up towards Pont-y-pair Bridge.

The Avenue Bettws-y-Coed.

**THE AVENUE**                                                           **No. 77**

This postcard shows the Hackney Carriages waiting to tout the visitors as they alight from the trains, etc. This stand is at the side of St Mary's Church. This card was bought in Betws and taken over to New York where it was sent to a lady who lived on 43-5th Avenue, New York.

78.

79.

## ST MARY'S CHURCH

Nos. 79, 80 & 82

St Mary's Church, built by Owen Gethin Jones, who also built the Railway Station. The church was opened in April 1873. As you can see in the top postcard, there is no clock tower. The church was built as a result of over crowding in the old St Michael's Church. The clock tower was finished in 1907, bottom postcard, and the clock was installed the same year. Generous benefactors from the village were Mr Charles Kurtz of Coed Celyn, Miss E. M. Evans of the Glan Aber, Colonel Johnstone of Coedfa, Mrs Elizabeth Emma Paterson and the Vicar himself, Rev J. W. Griffiths.

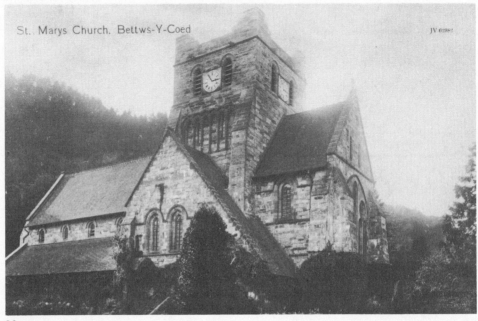

80.

## ST MICHAEL'S CHURCH                                    No. 81

The old church contains a tomb near the altar which represents a knight in armour. The inscription on the tomb is "Hic Jacet Gryffudd ab Davydd Goch Agnus Dei Miserere Mei", which translates "To the memory of Gruffydd ab Dafydd son to Dafydd Goch, natural son of Dafydd, brother of Llywelyn, the last Prince of Wales".

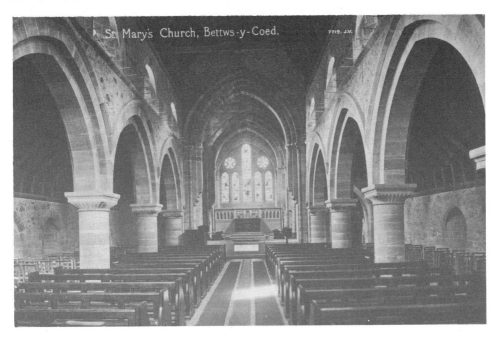

## INSIDE ST MARY'S CHURCH                               No. 82

The Font is constructed of Cornish serpentine stone, so also are the stones embodied with the sandstone in the pulpit. The bluestone of the Nave Walls have come from a local quarry.

**BRYN CONWAY** (1920s)                                                   No. 83

Advert stated "Behind St Mary's Church, central position, luncheons and teas, 3 reception rooms".
Proprietress: Mrs D. W. Evans.

84.                    The Roman Catholic Church is now on this site.

85.

# R. JONES,
## Confectioner, Baker, Grocer,
### And PROVISION DEALER,
## TEMPERANCE HOTEL,
(OPPOSITE THE ROAD LEADING FROM THE STATION,)
## TAN LAN, BETTWS-Y-COED.

DINNERS, TEAS, &c. ON THE SHORTEST NOTICE.

## Private Apartments.

PARTIES BOARDED BY THE DAY OR WEEK.
CHARGES STRICTLY MODERATE.

## TAN LAN, JUDGES & THE POST OFFICE                                    No. 86

Not much has changed since this photo was taken around 1940. Tan Lan is still there and is a family business which has been owned by the Parry's for many years. Next door is Judges who produced some of the best postcards of Betws and still do but moved their headquarters when a local man bought the premises from them and it is now a gift shop. The Post Office moved next door to Judges from its original location in the early 1900s.

## PENTRE DU VILLAGE                                                    No. 87

This postcard is a view looking towards the Village of Pentre Du.

**SOME MORE OF BETWS (1910s)**                                    No. 88

Looking towards the old Crosskeys Cottages which have now been converted to the Crosskeys Hotel and Restaurant.

**NEAR THE VILLAGE (1910s)**                                      No. 89

This postcard is taken up at Pentre Du, looking towards Miners Bridge. The first house on the left is Gorphwysfa, and then Bronant. On the right is one of Telford's milestones.

**PENTRE DU**   *(JUDGES POSTCARDS LTD. HASTINGS)*   No. 90

A mile from the centre of Betws on the A5 Holyhead road is the village of Pentre Du. This is where the Fire Station is situated and local volunteers are always on call.

**WELSH STALL**   No. 91

Jane Jones, in Welsh costume, at her stall at the Miners Bridge.
Details written on the back of the postcard . . .
"Went into Betws-y-coed yesterday and this old lady on the postcard served us from the little stall you see. She was a funny old soul. Aug. 18th 1911".

92.

# OAKFIELD

## BETTWS-Y-COED

Stands in its own grounds, close to Miner's Bridge and within easy distance of the far-famed Swallow Falls. Sanitation perfect. Motor House. Fishing, etc. Accommodation for Cyclists, Tourists and Motorists.

Terms with or without Board.

Special Terms for Large Parties.

Proprietress—Miss A. EVANS.

*NOW THE MINERS BRIDGE INN*

MINERS BRIDGE                                                        No. 93

This bridge was built by the miners of Rhiwddolion, a little deserted village of the 1700s which is up the Sarn Helen Roman road, which is on the opposite side to the Miners Bridge on the A5. This bridge has had about four alterations since around the 1800s. The Miners Bridge crosses the River Llugwy about a mile from Betws-y-coed on the A5 to Bangor. The bridge itself is a wooden ladder shaped structure and from it very beautiful views are to be obtained up and down the river.

## Tŷ HYLL                                                                                      No. 94

Tŷ Hyll (*The Ugly House*) is past the Swallow Falls on the way to Capel Curig. This house was built in one night, constructed entirely of local slate. Built according to the ancient laws of Hywel Dda in the tenth century A.D., whereby the house became the property of the bondman if it was completely built between sunset and sunrise and smoke from the fire emerged through the chimney before dawn.

## THE TOWERS                                                                                   No. 95

This house is an old fashioned, simple country residence set on a hillside 600 feet above sea level. It has glorious views of Moel Siabod, the Llugwy Valley and River.
This house is now an Outdoor Pursuit Centre.

SWALLOW FALLS HOTEL, BETTWS-Y-COED. 94908. JK.

96.

# Swallow Falls Hotel

One of the best and most beautifully situated hotels in North Wales. Replete with every comfort and everything to make the stay of visitors a complete joy from start to finish.

**BILLIARDS, TENNIS, POSTING AND FISHING.**
**IDEAL MOTORING CENTRE.**

# Bettws-y-Coed

Under the Personal Supervision of
P. A. MEREDITH :: Proprietor

*TERMS MODERATE.*

97.

98.

99.

100.

## SWALLOW FALLS

Nos. 100 & 101

Two miles from Betws-y-coed, on the Holyhead road (A5), brings you to the Swallow Falls (*Rhaeadr Ewynnol*), which have now become so famous they are visited by thousands of people annually. After viewing the upper falls, proceed down the steps to the lower falls and that is where you will really see and hear the beauty and roar of the Swallow Falls.

101.

"The Welsh Lady," Swallow Falls, Bettws-y-Coed

**WELSH LADY** No. 102

In the 1930s this young girl helped out at a stall at the Swallow Falls Hotel and would pose for photographers who would give her a small tip!

*Old Ellen-Lloyd* *+mas 190.3*
*ith much love wishing you a very Happy +mas*

**ELLEN LLOYD**　　　　　　　　　　　　　　　　　　　　　　　　**No. 103**

This is a postcard of one of the local lady's of Betws-y-coed again, dressed in typical Welsh costume, taken in the early 1900s. Many of the Betws postcards featuring Welsh Ladies have used local 'models' thereby making them quite historically interesting to modern-day locals. I love the big Welsh hat, it looks as though Ellen is in her Sunday best.

104.

"I hope you were 'carried away' by the delights of this place — Betws-y-coed".

105.

# MAP INDEX

| | |
|---|---|
| **A** | **BRYN AFON, Guest House** |
| **B** | **TAN DINAS, Guest House** |
| **C** | **SWALLOW FALLS HOTEL** |
| **D** | **MINERS BRIDGE INN**<br>**HENDRE CARAVAN SITE PARK** |
| **E** | **CROSSKEYS RESTAURANT & HOTEL** |
| **F** | **BOD HYFRYD, Guest House**<br>**RIVERSIDE HOTEL**<br>**CABAN-Y-PAIR CAFÉ**<br>**UPSTAIRS DOWNSTAIRS RESTAURANT** |
| **G** | **PONT-Y-PAIR HOTEL** |
| **H** | **ROYAL OAK HOTEL**<br>**ANNA DAVIES (Welsh Wool Shop)**<br>**PLAS DERWEN, Hotel**<br>**FAIRHAVEN HOTEL** |
| **I** | **COED-Y-FRON, Guest House**<br>**CHURCHILL, Guest House**<br>**BRYN CONWY, Guest House** |
| **J** | **TAN LAN, Restaurant**<br>**GWYDYR HOTEL**<br>**GLAN ABER HOTEL**<br>**JENNY JONES, Museum of Memories** |
| **K** | **THE FERNS, Guest House**<br>**MAELGWYN, Guest House** |
| **L** | **MOTOR MUSEUM**<br>**DILS DINER**<br>**LOG CABIN GIFT SHOP**<br>**TOURIST INFORMATION CENTRE** |
| **M** | **RIVERSIDE CARAVAN SITE PARK** |
| **N** | **PARK HILL HOTEL**<br>**BRYN BELLA, Guest House** |
| **O** | **TŶ GWYN HOTEL** |
| **P** | **CRAIG-Y-DDERWEN HOTEL** |
| **Q** | **CRAIG DINAS, Guest House**<br>**PENGWERN, Guest House** |
| **R** | **SILVER FOUNTAIN INN** |
| **S** | **CONWAY FALLS RESTAURANT** |
| **T** | **ROMAN BRIDGE** |
| **U** | **PANDY MILL** |
| **V** | **FAIRY GLEN HOTEL** |

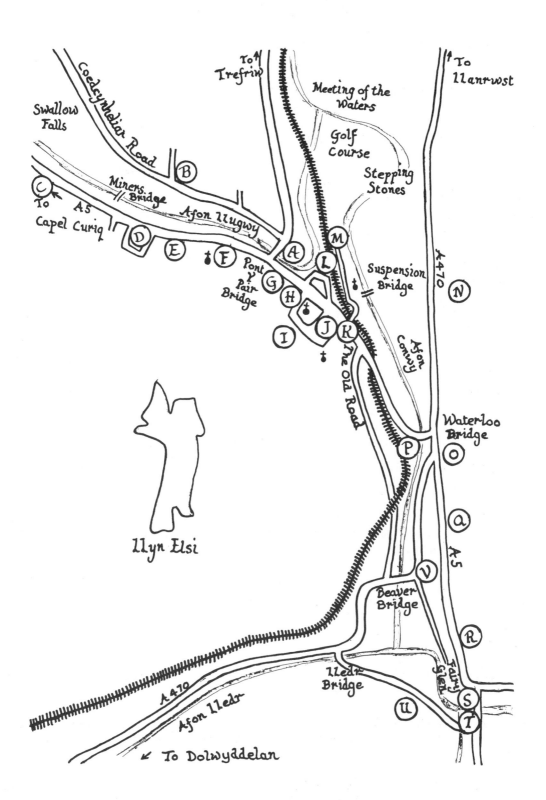

Swallow Falls

Coedcynhelier Road

To
Trefriw

To Llanrwst

Meeting of the Waters

Golf Course

Stepping Stones

B

C
To
Capel Curig

A5

Miners Bridge

Afon Llugwy

D

E

F

G

Pont Y Pair Bridge

H

I

J

K

A

L

M

N

A470

Suspension Bridge

Afon Conwy

The Old Road

Llyn Elsi

P

O

Waterloo Bridge

Q

A5

V

Beaver Bridge

R

A470

Afon Lledr

Lledr Bridge

Fairy Glen

U

S

T

← To Dolwyddelan

# WHERE TO STAY

All the Guest Houses and Hotels listed below offer excellent accommodation, just choose the location you would like to stay.

## GUEST HOUSES

**BRYN AFON**　　　　　　　　　　　　　　**MARION & BILL BETTENEY 710403**
Overlooking the Pont-y-pair Bridge and Falls.

**BRYN BELLA**　　　　　　　　　　　　**EILEEN & MASOOD FAKHRI 710627**
Overlooking the River Conwy and Village.

**BRYN CONWY**　　　　　　　　　　　　　　**HEFINA HUGHES 710239**
In the centre of the village behind Saint Mary's Church.

**BOD HYFRYD**　　　　　　　　　　　　　　**EVE EVELEIGH 710220**
Overlooking the River Llugwy and Clogwyn Cyrau.

**COED-Y-FRON**　　　　　　　　　　　　**FRANK & LOLA KELLY 710365**
Again, in the centre of the village behind St Mary's Church.

**CRAIG DINAS**　　　　　　　　　　　　　**EIRA & MICHAEL 710254**
Overlooking the Lledr Valley — panoramic views. Charming country house built 1920. Pets by prior arrangement.

**FERNS**　　　　　　　　　**KEITH & TERESA ROOBOTTOM 710587**
In the heart of the village looking up the Conwy Valley.

**MAELGWYN HOUSE**　　　　　　　　　　**DAVE & SUE WALSH 710252**
Again, in the heart of the village looking up the Conwy Valley.

**PENGWERN — W.T.B. 2 Crown Mint**　　　　　**SALLY & IVOR STEWART 710480**
Overlooking the Lledr Valley. Easy walks to the Fairy Glen and Conway Falls. All year for B & B. Evening Meal available.

**TAN DINAS**　　　　　　　　　　　　　**ANN HOWARD 710635**
A Guest House for non-smokers, overlooking the valley of River Llugwy.

## HOTELS

**CHURCH HILL PRIVATE HOTEL**　　　　**ALAN & DOROTHY FRENCH 710447**
Overlooking centre of village behind St Mary's Church.

**CRAIG-Y-DDERWEN — 3 Star 4 Crown**　　　　　**ENQUIRIES 710293**
Overlooking River Conwy. Catering for Weddings, Conferences, Parties. Accommodation of the highest calibre. Trendy Café Bar.

**CROSSKEYS HOTEL — 3 Crowns Tourist Board**　　　　**710334**
Overlooking the Llugwy River. A comfortable family run hotel with an excellent reputation for good food and value.

**FAIRY GLEN HOTEL**                                    JANET & GRAHAM BALL 710269
Overlooking Beaver Bridge near Fairy Glen. Excellent home cooked foods.

**FAIRHAVEN HOTEL**                                    MR & MRS J. O'CONNOR 710309
In the heart of the village. Private Hotel & Licensed Restaurant.

**GLAN ABER HOTEL**                                    MR & MRS GIDDINGS 710325
In the heart of the village. Recently modernised to high standard. Open fires. Renown friendly atmosphere. Room for lectures, etc. Golfing and Fishing by arrangement.

**GWYDYR HOTEL — 2 Star 4 Crown**            DAVID & OWEN WAINWRIGHT 710777
In the heart of village. The hotel has retained a Victorian look. Catering for functions, weddings, etc. Coffee Shop open all day.

**PARK HILL HOTEL**                                    JAMES & BETTY BOVAIRD 710540
On the road to Llanrwst overlooking the village. Private swimming pool.

**PLAS DERWEN HOTEL**                                    LEN & ANN WILLIAMS 710388
In the heart of the village overlooking River Llugwy. Licensed Restaurant.

**PONT-Y-PAIR HOTEL**                                    ENQUIRIES 710407
In the heart of the village overlooking the Pont-y-pair Bridge. Full menu available all day. Everyone made welcome.

**RIVERSIDE HOTEL**                                    LYNN & FIONA STILWELL 710650
In the heart of the village overlooking River Llugwy. Licensed restaurant.

**ROYAL OAK HOTEL — 3 Star**                                    ENQUIRIES 710219
Situated in the heart of Betws overlooking the River Llugwy. This very famous hotel is renowned for its excellent accommodation and food. Grill room open all day.

**SWALLOW FALLS HOTEL**                                    ENQUIRIES 710796
Overlooking the famous Swallow Falls. A favourite stop-over place with excellent function rooms. Live entertainment throughout the year.

**TŶ GWYN**                                    J. E. RATCLIFFE 710383
Overlooking the Waterloo Bridge. Winner of many awards for food and accommodation. Four Poster Beds in old world ambience of days past.

# INNS

**MINERS BRIDGE INN**                                    ENQUIRIES 710386
Panoramic views looking up the River Llugwy towards the Miners Bridge. Local pub with restaurant, bar meals and accommodation.

**SILVER FOUNTAIN INN**                                    ENQUIRIES 710341
Traditional inn near Conway Falls and Roman Bridge offering good food and real ale in cosy atmosphere. Families welcome.

# RESTAURANTS & CAFÉS

**CABAN-Y-PAIR CAFÉ**                                                    710505
Overlooking River Llugwy. Lunches served all day.

**CONWAY FALLS CAFÉ & RESTAURANT**                                      710696
Next to Conway Falls. All day breakfast plus an excellent Menu.

**DILS DINER**                                                          710346
Situated at the Railway Station. Coaches welcomed. Licensed, Self and Waitress Service. Mencap welcomed.

**TAN LAN**                                                             710232
Situated in the heart of the village. Open all day. Lunches, Teas. Cakes, Pastries and Bread are freshly baked on the premises.

# PLACES OF INTEREST

**ANNA DAVIES**                                                         710292
The Welsh Wool Shop for all your Gifts. Privately owned and personally managed.

**BETWS BUTTERFLY HOUSE**                                              710777
Free flying, magnificently coloured, exotic butterflies, in a tropical house.

**GWYDYR FISHING**                                                     710777
10 miles of Salmon Fishing, Gillie available. Excellent Sea Trout Fishing.

**HENDRE CARAVAN PARK, Holyhead Road, Pentre Du, Betws-y-coed.**
Situated at Pentre Du, near Miners Bridge. Tourist Caravans and Tents.

**LOG CABIN**                                                          710468
Welsh Gifts and Souveniers. Situated at the station approach.

**MOTOR MUSEUM**                                                       710632
A private collection of Vintage and Post Vintage Thoroughbred Cars. Bugatt Type 57, Aston Martin, M.G.s, Morgans, etc.

**MUSEUM OF MEMORIES (At Jenny Jones Gift Shop)**                       710260
Early 20th Century Costumes, Embroideries, Lacework, Memorabilia, etc.

**MOUNTAIN BIKE HIRE**                                                 710766
Situated behind Tan Lan Restaurant.

**MOUNTAIN GUIDE**                                                     710252
Dave Walsh, International Mountain Guide.

**PLAS-Y-BRENIN**                                                      06904 214
The National Mountain Centre at Capel Curig, 6 miles from Betws-y-coed. Mountaineering, Skiing, Canoeing, Orienteering or just go and see them.

**RIVERSIDE CARAVAN PARK**                                             710310
Situated near the old church of St Michaels. Tourist Caravans and Tents.

**TOURIST INFORMATION CENTRE**                                    710426

**TREFRIW WELLS SPA**                                    0492 640057
1.5 miles north of Trefriw Village towards Conwy on B5106. Visitor Centre open all year, 7 days per week. Guided Tours, Victorian Tea-rooms and shop. Producers of 'Spatone Plus', a supplement which is ideal to tone up your whole system, and the 'Spa' range of mineral rich natural hair and skin care products.

**UPSTAIRS DOWNSTAIRS RESTAURANT**                                    710424
Entertainment Room and Video Hire.

# BETWS-Y-COED

Betws-y-coed is a jewel set in the heart of North Wales
For peace and quiet you will find it in the hills and vales
The Swallow Falls cascades down the glen
A pleasure to be seen over and over again

Fairy Glen is an artist's dream
You gaze in wonder at this marverllous scene
Which ever road you travel along the way
You find the scenery more magnificent every day

The mountains of Snowdonia are a breath taking view
Woodland and rivers you find something new
Nature's beauty is all around
No better scenery can be found

Betws-y-coed is a pleasure to visit
For wildlife and nature there's everything in it
For a tourist attraction it leads the rest
It is a treasure of Wales for being the best.

*Jean Sandiford 1992*
*Author's Mother*

# FURTHER INFORMATION

**BOOKINGS** taken for **SLIDE SHOW TALKS** — on Betws-y-coed and Butterflies.

**POSTCARDS** — enlarged copies available on some of the postcards.

**COMMISSIONS** — The history of your Hotel, etc., displayed in a frame with old photographs and calligraphic writing.

**ARTEFACTS** — We are interested in purchasing any photographs and artefacts on Betws-y-coed.

**TRANSLATIONS** — We will arrange to have the book translated into the language of your choice if more than 1,000 copies required.

We hope you have enjoyed the book and will, at a later date, join us on our next Pictorial Trip Down Memory Lane.


**BOOK** — Further copies of the book are available from:-
Country Cottage Publications
Bryn Tirion
Miners Bridge
Betws-y-coed
LL24 0DA